HUMILITY,

THE BEAUTY OF HOLINESS

Rev. Andrew Murray

Lord Jesus! may our Holiness be perfect Humility!
Let Thy perfect Humility be our Holiness!

First published in 1895 by Fleming Revell Co.

The source text is in the public domain but this translation and accompanying editorial materials constitute original intellectual property © 2025 by Pastor Joe Lighthall.

Permission is required for reuse, reproduction, or distribution of this translated edition.

All rights reserved.

ISBN 978-1-918219-47-0

This Edition: December 2025

Published by: Cosmic Jive Publishing
www.cosmicjivepublishing.com

For permissions and inquiries, contact:
info@cosmicjivepublishing.com

WHY THIS BOOK NEEDED A FRESH VOICE

Andrew Murray's *Humility* is, quite simply, one of the most searching, convicting, and life-changing books ever written on the subject of pride, self, and the beauty of knowing Christ.

Murray shows, with relentless biblical clarity, that pride is the root of every sin and that true humility —the humility of the One who emptied Himself and took the form of a servant—is the beginning of all real life in God.

It lifts the human heart out of the spotlight of self-admiration and places it gently, firmly, at the feet of Jesus.

Pastors, missionaries, and ordinary believers have testified for over a century that this book shattered their illusions, exposed their egos, and led them into deeper fellowship with Christ. Few writings have so quietly shaped generations of servants who chose obscurity over applause, lowliness over influence, and the cross over the crown.

Yet most people today never finish it. The reason is not the message; the message is electric, even dangerous. The barrier is the packaging: long Victorian paragraphs, sentences that stretch across half a page, and words that have drifted out of daily use. Even devoted readers with years of Bible study often find themselves re-reading the same section again and again, losing the thread, and finally closing the book—robbed of the very grace God wanted to give them through it.

That is why this new edition exists. Every word of Murray's original argument remains—nothing added, nothing removed, nothing softened. The Scriptures he quoted are unchanged. The only thing that has changed is the voice: clear, contemporary English with shorter sentences and paragraphs that let the truth strike with the full force Murray intended.

Now a new generation can read without tripping. And when they do, they discover that Murray's words, once unlocked, still burn as brightly and cut as sharply as they did in 1895.

In a world obsessed with visibility, personal branding, and being "known," this book is countercultural to the bone. It will feel like rebellion. It will feel like relief.

My prayer is that this fresh voice will do for readers today what a fresh wind does to a sail: carry Christ's call to lowliness farther, faster, and deeper into hearts that are tired of performing and hungry for His presence.

May the same Holy Spirit who first moved Andrew Murray now use these updated words to set thousands more free from the tyranny of self and free for the unspeakable joy of being nothing—so that Jesus may be everything.

Pastor Joe Lighthall, Dec. 2025

Foreword to the Modern Edition

In an age when personal worth is measured in followers, valuations, and net-worth statements, when every achievement is expected to be announced, optimized, and monetized, Andrew Murray's book on humility lands like a quiet revolution.

You do not need another book on how to get richer, louder, or more visible. You need a book on how to become small enough for God to fill, quiet enough to hear Him, and low enough to serve others without needing credit.

This book is not a strategy for success as the world counts success; it is a pathway to the only success that will matter when the likes fade and the accounts are closed.

Read it slowly. Read it suspiciously—your ego will hate it. Read it prayerfully, because humility is not a trait we can manufacture; it is a grace we receive in the presence of Jesus, "who humbled Himself by becoming obedient to the point of death, even death on a cross."

In a world addicted to self-elevation, may this timeless book teach a new generation the secret: the way up is down.

JL, 2025

A Note from the Editor

Every chapter, every section, every biblical quotation is here in the same order as the original. Nothing has been removed, added, or softened. What has changed is only the presentation:

- The Victorian-era language has been carefully rewritten in clear, contemporary English so today's readers can immediately grasp Murray's full message.
- Roman numerals have been replaced with ordinary numbers.
- Long, dense paragraphs have been broken into shorter ones for modern eyes
- All Bible quotations are retained in the wording Murray himself used, because those precise shades of meaning matter.

The meaning, the challenge, and the power of the original words remain exactly the same — only now they are easier to read, to share and to apply.

PREFACE

There are three big reasons which urge us to be full of humility. Humility is the attitude that is the best fit for someone, from the perspective of them being 1) a creature—that is a created being, 2) a sinner, and 3) a saint.

AS A CREATED BEING—a creature under the creator.

The first big reason for having humility is seen in the angels, in unfallen man, and in the Lord Jesus as the Son of Man.

AS A SINNER.

The second big reason for having humility meets us in our fallen state. It shows that the only way back to our true place as a created being is the way of the deepest humility and repentance.

AS A SAINT.

In the third big reason for having humility, we encounter the mystery of grace. This teaches us that as we let ourselves be lost in the vast greatness of God's redeeming love, humility becomes for us the height of eternal happiness and worship.

In our usual religious teaching, the second big reason has been emphasized far too much, to the point that some people have even gone so far as to say that we must keep sinning if we are truly to stay humble.

Others have thought that strong self-condemnation is the real secret of humility. But the Christian life has suffered where believers have not been clearly taught that as created beings under the creator, nothing is more natural, beautiful, or blessed than to be nothing so that God may be everything.

The Christian life has suffered whenever it is not clearly taught that it is grace—not sin—that humbles us most.

A soul that is led to recognize its own sinfulness and then focuses on God in His wonderful glory as God, Creator, and Redeemer is the soul that will truly bow lowest before Him.

In this book I have, for several reasons, focused almost entirely on the humility that is fitting for us as created beings. This is not only because the link between humility and sin is emphasized so much already in Christian teaching, but also because I believe that, for the Christian life to be fully lived, this other aspect must be given far greater prominence.

If Jesus is truly to be our example in humility in His humility and lowliness, we need to understand the principles on which His humility was founded. These principles form the common ground we share with Him, and it is through these principles which our likeness to Him is to be achieved.

If we are truly to be humble—not only before God but also toward other people—and if humility is to become our joy, we must understand that humility is not only a sign of shame because of being a sinner.

We will see that humility is a way of being clothed with the very beauty and blessedness of heaven and of Jesus Himself.

We will see that just as Jesus found His glory in taking the form of a servant, so when He told us, "Whoever wants to be first among you must be your servant," He was simply teaching us a wonderful truth: there is nothing so godly, nothing so heavenly, as being the servant and helper of everyone around us.

A faithful servant who understands his role actually finds real pleasure in meeting the needs of his master or his master's guests. When we recognize that humility is infinitely deeper than remorse and sorrow over sin, and when we accept humility as our share in the participation in the life of Jesus, we begin to see that humility is our true royal calling as children of the king.

And as we learn to live humility out by becoming the servants of all, proving our royal natures by our humble acts of service and attitude, we discover that this is the highest fulfillment of our destiny as people created in the image of God— as children of the king.

When I look back on my own spiritual journey, and then look around at Jesus's Church in the world today, I am struck—and honestly amazed—by how little humility is sought after by Christians. I am struck by how little humility is wanted by Christians in their lives or manifest there.

Humility shows the church and the world that someone is Jesus' real disciple. Humility is the defining sign of being a disciple of Jesus. But it is not valued, desired or wanted today.

In our preaching and our living, in the everyday interactions of home and social life, in our fellowship with other believers, and even in the planning and carrying out of work for Christ—there is, sadly, so much evidence that humility is not valued as a prime fruit or Christian quality.

Humility is not treated by believers today as the one essential root from which all other spiritual gifts and fruits grow, nor is it treated as the one essential condition for genuine fellowship with Jesus. Humility is absolutely necessary.

Certain people in the church claim to be pursuing "higher holiness" and they make claims to be holy. However, others say of them that despite their loud claims, their characters have not been marked by a growing humility. This is a concern and should serve as a loud alarm call to every sincere Christian.

Whatever the truth is behind their detractors' claims, and even the 'higher holiness' people's own claims for that matter, whether they are truly holy or humble or not, the fact that they are accused of this urges us to show the world that meekness, humility and lowliness of heart really are the main signs by which the followers of the meek and lowly and humble Lamb of God are to be recognized.

1
Humility: The Glory of the Creature

'They shall cast their crowns before the throne, saying: Worthy art Thou, our Lord and our God, to receive the glory, and the honour and the power: for Thou didst create all things, and because of Thy will they were, and were created.'—REV. 4: 11.

WHEN GOD created the universe, His one purpose was to allow His creatures to share in His own holiness, perfection and blessedness. In doing so, He intended that all creation would display the glory of His love, wisdom, and power.

God desired to reveal Himself in and through the beings He made by giving them as much of His own goodness and glory as they were able to receive.

His goal was not merely to hand His creature some independent store of life or spiritual gift or power—something they could possess in itself, or control all on their own. Not at all. Because God is the ever-living, ever-present, ever-active One—the One who sustains all things by His powerful word, the One in whom everything exists. Therefore, the creature's relationship to God could only ever be one of constant, absolute, all-encompassing dependence.

As truly as God once created everything by His power, so just as truly must He keep and sustain everything at every moment by that same power.

The creature must look back to its origin, to its beginning, and admit that it owes everything entirely to God.

The creature's greatest concern, its highest calling, and its real happiness—now and for all eternity—is to offer itself as an empty vessel in which God's life can live and through. An empty vessel through which He can reveal His power and goodness.

The life and spirit God gives is not something imparted once and then left for us to manage on our own. It is given continually, moment by moment, through the constant working of His mighty power.

Because of this, humility—that is our posture of complete dependence on God—is, by the very nature of things, the creature's first duty and highest calling. It is also the root of every other gift, fruit and calling.

Therefore pride, or us losing sight of this humility and not acting it out, is the root of every sin and every evil.

It was when the now fallen angels began to admire themselves with self-satisfaction that they were led into disobedience and were cast out from the light of heaven into outer darkness.

In the same way, when the serpent breathed the poison of his pride—the desire to be as God—into the hearts of our first parents, they too fell from their high position into all the misery in which humanity ass now fallen.

In both heaven and earth, pride and self-exaltation are the gate, the birth, and the curse of hell. (See Note A at the back of this book.) Therefore, it follows that real redemption must restore the humility mankind once lost—the original and only true relationship a creature can have to its God.

And so Jesus came to bring humility back to earth, to make us sharers in it, and to save us by it.

In heaven, He humbled Himself by becoming a man. The humility we see in Him on earth already belonged to Him in heaven; it brought Him here, and He brought it with Him from heaven.

Here on earth, Jesus 'humbled Himself and became 'obedient even to death'. His humility gave His death its power and worth, and in this way His humility became our redemption.

And now the salvation He gives us is nothing less —and nothing other—than sharing His own life and death, His own character and spirit, His own humility. This humility is the foundation of His relationship to God and the root of His redeeming work and should be ours as His followers too.

Jesus Christ took humanity's place and fulfilled our destiny as creatures through His own life of perfect humility. His humility is our salvation. His salvation is our humility.

And so the life of Christians who are saved—the

saints, those ones who are set apart for God—must carry this sign of deliverance from sin and this sign of a full restoration to mankind's original condition. This sign being that the Christian's entire relationship to both God and people is shaped — and must be shaped — by humility. A humility that is deep and genuine and which influences everything the person is and everything they do. Not just with God but with others.

Without this humility, there can be no true abiding in God's presence, no real experience of His favor and power of His Spirit. Without this humility, there can be no lasting faith, no lasting love, no lasting joy, and no lasting strength.

Humility is the only soil in which the gifts and fruits of the Spirit can take root and then flourish. The absence of humility is enough to explain every defect, every failure and every weakness.

Humility is not so much a gift or fruit like the other gifts or fruits; it is the root of all the gifts and fruits, because only humility places us in the right attitude before God and allows Him, as God, to do all.

God gave us the ability to think, and He designed us so that the better we understand what a command truly means and why it is absolutely necessary, the more willing and complete our obedience to that command will be. That's how it should be.

The call to humility has been overlooked in the Church largely because its real nature and importance have not been really understood.

Humility

Humility is not something we offer to God, nor something He hands to us as a separate gift. Humility is simply the awareness of our complete nothingness that comes when we see how entirely God is everything. And in that awareness we make room for Him to be all.

When the creature recognises that this is what being a child of the king really means, and willingly becomes—with his or her will, mind, and affections—the mould and vessel in which the life and glory of God may act and reveal itself, then the creature sees that humility is simply admitting the truth of their position as a creature under the Most High and yielding to God His rightful place.

In the lives of sincere Christians——those who seek holiness and claim to pursue it—humility should be the main sign of their sincerity. It is often said that this is not the case. One reason may be that, in the Church's teaching and example, humility has not been given the supreme importance that belongs to it.

And this neglect may spring from overlooking the deeper truth that, powerful as the awareness of our sin may be in motivating an attitude of humility, there is an even bigger influence: the very thing that makes the angels humble, that made Jesus humble, and that makes the holiest saints in heaven humble. This is the realization that the first and greatest sign of the creature's relationship to God—the secret of the creature's happiness and well-being—is the humility and nothingness that leaves God free to be all.

I am sure many Christians would admit that their experience has been much like my own in this: we had known the Lord for a long time without realizing that meekness, humility and lowliness of heart are meant to be the distinguishing marks of a disciple, just as they were the distinguishing marks of our Master.

And more than that, we often assumed humility would just simply appear on its own after our conversion. But true humility does not come naturally even to Christians; it must be something they deliberately seek—something they desire, pray for, trust God for, and practice.

As we study Scripture, we begin to see how clear and how often repeated Jesus' instructions on humility were, and yet how slow His disciples were to understand Him.

Let us recognize, right at the beginning of this book, that nothing is so natural to human beings, nothing works so subtly and hides itself so deeply, and nothing is so difficult and dangerous, as pride.

Let us take to heart that only a steady, persistent waiting on God and on Christ can reveal to us how much we lack the grace of humility, and how powerless we are to produce real humility in ourselves.

Let us keep our eyes fixed on the character of Christ until our hearts are filled with love for Him and admiration for His humility and lowliness.

And let us trust that when we are humbled—when we finally feel the weight of our pride and recognize our inability to remove it—Jesus Christ

Humility

Himself will come and give us this humility in us as well. He will impart His humility to us as part of His own wonderful life working within and through us.

2
Humility: the Secret of Redemption

'Have this mind in you which was also in Christ Jesus: who emptied Himself; taking the form of a servant; and humbled Himself; becoming obedient even unto death. Wherefore God also highly exalted Him.'
—PHIL. 2: 5-7.

NO TREE CAN GROW away from the root that gave it life. Throughout its entire life it can only live by the same life that was in the seed from which it sprang. Fully grasping this truth —both in relation to the first Adam and to the Second Adam—can greatly help us understand both the need for redemption and the nature of the redemption Jesus brings.

The Need: When the Old Serpent—the one cast out of heaven for his pride, whose very nature as the devil is pride—spoke his tempting words into Eve's ear, those words carried the very poison of hell with them. And when Eve listened, allowing her desire and her will to yield to the prospect of becoming as God, knowing good and evil, that poison entered her soul, her blood, and her life. That poison destroyed forever the blessed humility and dependence on God that would have been our own everlasting happiness.

In its place, Eve's life—and the life of the whole human race that came from her—became corrupted at its very root by the most terrible of all sins and curses: the poison of Satan's own pride.

All the misery that has ever filled the world—its wars and the bloodshed among nations, its selfishness and suffering, its ambitions and jealousies, its broken hearts and embittered lives, its daily unhappiness—can be traced back to what this dreadful, hell-born pride has brought about, whether in ourselves or in others.

It was pride that made redemption necessary. Above everything else, it is pride from which we must be redeemed. And our understanding of our need for redemption will depend largely on how clearly we see the terrible nature of this power of pride that has entered our very being.

No tree can grow away from the root that first produced it. The power Satan brought from hell and injected into human life is at work every day, every hour, with tremendous force throughout the world. People suffer because of it; they fear it, they resist it, they run from it—yet they do not know where it comes from or how it gained such terrible control and dominance. And because people do not know its source, it is no surprise that they have no idea where to turn or how to overcome it.

Pride has its root and strength in a fearsome spiritual power, operating both inside us and outside us. It is necessary not only that we confess and mourn over our pride as something that is our own, owning it as something that lives within us, but that we recognize its origin in Satan himself.

If this understanding about pride drives us to utter despair about ever conquering or removing it by our own efforts, then this knowledge of our own helplessness will only bring us more quickly to the supernatural power in which our true deliverance lies—the redemption brought by the Lamb of God.

The struggle against the workings of self and pride within us may feel hopeless enough, but when we realize that a power of darkness stands behind it, it feels even more hopeless. Yet that utter despair — the realization we are really what we are and helpless—this then enables us to better receive and rely on a power and a life outside of ourselves. This power is nothing less than the humility of heaven itself, brought to us by the Lamb of God to overthrow Satan and his pride.

No tree can grow away from the root that first produced it. In the same way that we must look to the first Adam and his fall to understand the power of sin within us, we must also look to the Second Adam and His power to establish within us a life of humility—one as real, continuous, and dominant as pride has been in us.

We receive our life from and in Christ as truly, indeed even more truly, than from and in Adam. We are called to walk 'rooted' in Christ, 'holding fast the Head from whom the whole body increaseth with the increase of God.'

The life of God entered human nature in the

incarnation of Jesus Christ when he was born as the son of Mary. This same life of God is the root in which we are meant to stand and grow and flourish. This life of God is the same almighty power that worked in Christ, and carried Christ through death to resurrection. This same mighty life and power now works in us day by day.

Our one great need is to study, understand, trust, and surrender to the life demonstrated in and revealed in Christ—the life and power that is now ours, waiting only for our willing permission and consent so that the life of God may take full possession and mastery of our entire being.

From this perspective, it is immensely important that we think rightly about who Christ is—about what truly makes Him the Christ—and think especially about what can be considered His defining characteristic, the very root and essence of His nature as our Redeemer.

There can be but one answer: it is His humility.

What is the incarnation, except His heavenly humility—His willingness to empty Himself and become human?

What is His life on earth, except humility—His choosing to take the form of a servant?

And what is His atonement, except humility—"He humbled Himself and became obedient unto death"?

And what is His ascension and glory, except humility raised to the throne and crowned with honour? "He humbled Himself; therefore God highly exalted Him."

Whether in heaven with the Father, in His birth, in His earthly life, in His death, or in His enthronement, it is all humility—nothing but humility.

Christ is the humility of God expressed in human nature: the Eternal Love humbling itself, wrapping itself in meekness and gentleness in order to win us, serve us, and save us.

Because God's love and willingness to stoop down make Him the one who blesses, helps, and serves everyone, Jesus had to be the very embodiment of humility when He became human. And He still is—standing at the center of the throne as the humble and meek Lamb of God.

If this is the root of the tree, then its nature must show itself in every branch, leaf, and fruit. If humility is the first and all-encompassing grace in the life of Jesus—if humility is the very secret of His atonement—then the health and strength of our spiritual lives will depend entirely on us putting humility first as well.

We must make humility the main thing we admire in Jesus, the main thing we seek from Jesus, and the one thing for which we are willing to give up everything else. (See Note B at rear of this volume.)

Is it any wonder that the Christian life is so often weak and without fruit when the very root of Christ's own life is neglected or not even unknown?

And is it any wonder that the joy of salvation is so rarely felt, when the very thing in which Christ Himself found joy—and through which He brings joy to us—is so rarely sought after?

Humility

Until we desire a humility that will settle for nothing less than the ending and dying of self; a humility that, like Jesus, gives up all human praise in order to seek only the honor that comes from God; a humility that counts itself absolutely nothing so that God may be everything and the Lord alone may be exalted—until such humility becomes what we look for in Christ above every other joy, and what we welcome at any cost—there is little hope of a Christianity that will truly overcome the world.

I must plead earnestly with you: if you have not seriously considered before how much humility is lacking within you or those around you, pause now and look closely. Ask yourself whether you truly see the spirit of the humble, meek and lowly Lamb of God in those who bear His name.

Consider how every failure of love, every indifference to the needs, feelings, or weaknesses of others, every sharp judgment or harsh word—so often excused under the idea of being honest or straightforward—every flare of temper or irritation, every trace of bitterness or estrangement, all spring from nothing but pride, which always seeks its own way. If you look steadily at this, your eyes will begin to see how a dark—should I not say devilish—pride slips in almost everywhere, the gatherings of the saints being no exception.

Then ask yourself what would happen if, in yourself and among believers around you, in your dealings with fellow-Christians and with the world, hearts were truly and consistently guided by the humility of Jesus. Wouldn't the cry of our whole being, day and night, become, "Oh, for the humility of Jesus in me and in all others around me!"?

Let your heart face honestly your own lack of the kind of humility revealed through Christ's life and in the whole character of His redeeming work. When you do, you may feel as though you have never truly understood what Christ and His salvation really are.

Study the humility of Jesus. This is the secret, the hidden root of your redemption. Sink into it more deeply each day. Believe with your whole heart that this Jesus Christ—whose divine humility accomplished your salvation—will come to dwell and work within you as well, and will shape you into what the Father desires you to be.

3
The Humility of Jesus

'I am in the midst of you as he that serveth.'
— Luke 22:26

IN THE GOSPEL OF JOHN, the inner life of our Lord is laid open to us and revealed. Jesus often speaks about His own relationship with the Father—the motives that guide Him, the awareness He has of the power and Spirit in which He acts.

Even though the word "humble" does not appear in John's gospel, nowhere else in Scripture do we see so clearly what Jesus' humility truly was. John's gospel reveals Christ's humility.

We have already said that humility, in its essence, is simply the creature agreeing to let God be everything, surrendering entirely to His working.

In Jesus, we shall see how—both as the Son of God in heaven and as a man on earth—He willingly took the place of complete submission, giving God the honor and glory that belong to Him alone. Jesus on earth agreed to let God be everything, surrendering Himself entirely to His working.

And we shall see that what Jesus taught so often became perfectly true in His own life: "He that humbleth himself shall be exalted." As Scripture declares, "He humbled Himself; therefore God highly exalted Him."

Listen to how our Lord speaks about His relationship with the Father—notice how constantly He uses the words not and nothing about Himself. The "not I" with which Paul later describes his life in Christ is the very spirit of what Christ says about His own life in relation to the Father.

- The Son can do nothing of Himself (John 5:19).
- I can of My own self do nothing; My judgment is just because I seek not My own will (John 5:30).
- I receive not glory from men (John 5:41).
- I am come not to do My own will (John 6:38).
- My teaching is not Mine (John 7:16).
- I am not come of Myself (John 7:28).
- I do nothing of Myself (John 8:28).
- I have not come of Myself, but He sent Me (John 8:42).
- I seek not My own glory (John 8:50).
- The words I speak, I speak not from Myself (John 14:10).
- The word you hear is not Mine (John 14:24).

These words reveal the deepest roots of Christ's life and work. They tell us how Almighty God was able to carry out His great work of redemption through Him.

These words show us what Jesus believed was the

proper state of heart for the Son in relation to the Father.

And these words reveal the essential nature of the redemption Christ accomplished and now shares with us. It is this: He made Himself nothing so that God might be everything. He surrendered Himself —His will, His abilities, His glory—entirely to the Father's working.

Of His own power, His own will, His own honour, His entire mission with all its works and teaching, Jesus said: It is not I. I am nothing. I have given Myself to the Father to work. I am nothing; the Father is all.

This life of complete self-denial, of absolute submission and dependence on the Father's will, was for Christ a life of perfect peace and joy. He lost nothing by giving everything to God. God honored His trust, accomplished all things through Him, and afterwards exalted Him to His own right hand in glory.

And because Christ had humbled Himself before God, keeping God always before Him, He was able to humble Himself before people as well, and to be the Servant of all.

His humility was simply His surrender of Himself to God, allowing God to do in Him whatever He pleased, no matter what people around Him might think or say or do.

It is in this state of mind and heart, that the redeeming power of Christ lies. We are made partakers of Christ, sharers in Him, to bring us into this same state of mind and heart. This is the true self-denial to which our Saviour calls us: the recognition that self has no good in it except as an empty vessel that God must fill, and that any claim of self to be or do anything must not be admitted for a moment.

It is in this, above everything else, that conformity to Jesus consists—the being and doing nothing of ourselves, so that God may be all.

Here we find the root and nature of true humility. It is because this is so little understood or sought after that our humility is shallow and weak. We must learn from Jesus how He is humble, meek and lowly of heart. He teaches us that true humility begins and finds its strength in the understanding that God works all in all, and that our place is to yield to Him in complete resignation and dependence, fully consenting to be and to do nothing of ourselves.

This is the life Christ came to reveal and to give us—a life toward God that came through death to sin and self. If we feel that such a life is too high for us and beyond our reach, this should only make us seek it the more earnestly in Him; for it is Christ dwelling within who lives this humble, meek and lowly life in us.

If we long for this, then above all else let us seek the holy secret of knowing the nature of God as the One who at every moment works all things in all creatures. Let us learn the secret that all creation, every creature, and above all every child of God, is simply a vessel, a channel through which the living God can reveal the riches of His wisdom, power, and goodness.

The root of all spiritual maturity, spiritual power, spiritual gifts and grace, of all faith and true worship, lies in knowing that we have nothing except what we receive from God, and in bowing in deepest humility to wait upon God for it.

It was because this humility was not merely a passing feeling—something stirred up when He happened to think of God—but this humility was the very spirit of His entire life, that Jesus was as humble in His dealings with people as He was in His communion with God. He saw Himself as God's Servant for the sake of those whom God had made and loved; and naturally, He regarded Himself as the Servant of people, so that through Him God might carry out His work of love.

He never once thought of seeking His own honor or using His power to defend or vindicate Himself. His whole attitude was that of a life yielded to God, allowing God to work in Him.

We as Christians will not feel the weight of how little true, heavenly, and visible humility there is among us, and we will not grieve for it, until we learn to see the humility of Jesus as the very heart of His redeeming work, until we see it as the true joy of the Son's life, and the only right way to relate to the Father—and as something He must give us if we are to share in Him at all.

Only then will we be willing to set aside our usual religious habits in order to seek humility above everything else: the first and greatest evidence that Christ lives in us.

Are you living in humility? Ask your daily life.

Ask Jesus Himself. Ask your friends. Ask the world. And begin even now to thank God that, in Jesus, a heavenly humility has been opened to you—a humility you may hardly have understood or experienced—and through it a heavenly blessing you possibly may never have tasted can come into you.

4
Humility in the Teaching of Jesus

'Learn of Me, for I am meek and lowly of heart."—Matthew 11:29.

Whosoever will be chief among you, let him be your servant, even as the Son of Man came to serve.'—Matthew 20:27.

WE HAVE SEEN HUMILITY in the life of Christ, as He allowed us to look into His heart. Now let us listen to His teaching. There we hear how He speaks of humility, and how fully He expects people—especially His disciples—to be humble as He was.

Let us look carefully at the passages, which I can scarcely do more than quote, so we may feel the full weight of how often and how earnestly Jesus taught humility. Doing so may help us grasp what He truly asks of us.

1. At the very beginning of His ministry, in the Beatitudes that open the Sermon on the Mount, Jesus says: 'Blessed are the poor in spirit; for theirs is the kingdom of heaven. Blessed are the meek; for they shall inherit the earth.'

His first words about the kingdom of heaven reveal the only way to get there. The poor in spirit—

the ones who know they have nothing in themselves—receive the kingdom. The meek—the ones who do not seek anything in themselves—will inherit the earth.

The blessings of heaven and earth are for the lowly. In both the heavenly life and the earthly one, humility is the secret to blessing.

2. 'Learn of Me; for I am meek and lowly of heart, and ye shall find rest for your souls.'

Jesus offers Himself as our Teacher. He tells us clearly what spirit we will find in Him and what He desires to give to us.

Meekness of character and a humble mindset—this is the one thing He offers, and in receiving it we find true rest for our deepest selves.

Humility is to be a salvation.

3. When the disciples had been arguing over which of them would be greatest in the kingdom—and even brought the question to Jesus (Luke 9:46; Matt. 18:3)—He placed a little child in their midst and said, 'Whosoever shall humble himself as this little child, shall be exalted.'

Their question, "Who is the greatest in the kingdom of heaven?" reaches deeply into the very nature of that kingdom. What is the highest honor there? What is heaven's true nobility? No one but Jesus could have given such an answer in reply: the chief glory of heaven, the essence of being heavenly-minded, the best of all the fruits, is humility. "He that is least among you—this one is great."

4. The sons of Zebedee had asked Jesus to let them sit at His right and left—positions of highest honor in the kingdom. Jesus answered that these places were not His to give, but the Father's, who would assign them to those for whom they were prepared. They were not to seek them or even to desire them. Their minds needed instead to be fixed on the "cup" and the "baptism" of humility.

And then He added, 'Whosoever will be chief among you, let him be your servant. Even as the Son of Man came to serve.'

Humility, as it is the defining characteristic of the heavenly Christ, will also be the defining characteristic of glory in heaven.

The one who is most humble is the one closest to God.

The highest position in the Church belongs to the humblest person.

5. Speaking to the crowds and to His disciples about the Pharisees and their love of the places of honor, Christ repeated the same truth (Matt. 23:11): 'He that is greatest among you shall be your servant.'

Humbling ourselves is the only way to get honor in God's kingdom.

6. On another occasion, while dining in a Pharisee's home, Jesus gave the parable of the wedding guest who is invited to move to a higher, more prestigious seat closer to the groom (Luke 14:1–11). And He concluded with the unchanging law of the kingdom:

For whosoever exalteth himself shall be abased; and he that humbleth himself shall be exalted.'

The demand is absolute—there is no other way. Only those who choose self-abasement will be lifted up.

7. After telling the parable of the Pharisee and the tax collector, Jesus said again (Luke 18:14), Everyone that exalteth himself shall be abased; and he that humbleth himself shall be exalted.'

In the temple, in the presence of God, and in our worship of Him, anything that is not soaked through by deep, genuine humility—toward both God and people—is worthless.

8. After Jesus washed the disciples' feet, He said (John 13:14), 'If I then, the Lord and Master, have washed your feet, ye also ought to wash one another's feet.'

His command, His example, and every thought connected with obeying Him or becoming like Him all insist on one thing: humility is the first and most essential part of being His disciple.

9. Even at the Last Supper, the disciples were still arguing about who among them was the greatest (Luke 22:26). Jesus answered, 'He that is greatest among you, let him be as the younger; and he that is chief, as he that doth serve. I am among you as he that serveth.'

The path Jesus walked—and the path He opened for us to follow on—is marked at every step by humility. It is the power and spirit through which He accomplished salvation, and the very spirit into which He intends to save us: the humility that makes us servants of all.

How rarely this is preached. How rarely it is practiced. How rarely we even notice or admit how little of it we have. I am not speaking only of how few people achieve some noticeable resemblance to Jesus in His humility—though that is true. I mean how few even think of making humility a deliberate, continual aim of desire, prayer, and pursuit. How little the world has seen of it. How little it has even been seen within the inner circles of the Church.

'Whosoever will be chief among you, let him be your servant.'

May God help us truly believe that Jesus meant exactly what He said!

We all know what characterizes a faithful servant or slave: a devotion to the master's interests, a thoughtful and considered examination and study of what makes their master happy, and a desire to please him, a delight in his success, honor, and happiness. There have been servants on earth who have shown these qualities so clearly that the very name "servant" has been their glory.

Many of us have discovered a new joy in the Christian life when we learned that we may give ourselves to God as His servants—His slaves—and that His service is our highest freedom, freedom from sin and from self.

Now we must learn another lesson: Jesus calls us to be servants to one another as well. And as we accept this calling willingly with our whole hearts, we will find that this too becomes a service that blesses us—a deeper freedom from sin and from self.

At first, it may feel difficult; this is only because pride still makes us think we are something. But once we grasp that being nothing before God is the glory of every creature, the spirit of Jesus, and the joy of heaven, then we will gladly embrace whatever discipline comes through serving even those who may even irritate or oppose us.

When our hearts are set on true sanctification, on true holiness, we will study every word Jesus spoke about self-abasement and humbling ourselves with new eagerness. No place will seem too low, no stooping too deep, no service too insignificant or too prolonged, if by it we may share and demonstrate fellowship with Him who said, "I am among you as one who serves."

Brothers and sisters, this is the path to the higher life: Down—lower down! This is what Jesus always said to the disciples when they dreamed of greatness in the kingdom or of sitting on His right or left hand. Do not seek or ask for exaltation—that is God's work. Your concern is this: humble yourselves. Take no position before God or people except that of a servant. That is your work; let it be your one purpose and prayer.

God is faithful. Just as water always seeks and fills the lowest place, so the moment God finds a soul humbled and emptied, His glory and power flow in to lift up and to bless. He who humbles himself—that must be our one concern—shall be exalted—that is God's concern. By His mighty power and His great love, He will definitely do it.

People sometimes suggest that humility and meekness take away what is noble, bold, and truly manlike in us. If only everyone would believe that humility is a sign of a royal child of the kingdom of heaven! This is the royal spirit the King of heaven Himself displayed. That this is what is Godlike: to humble oneself, to become the servant of all. This is the path to the joy and glory of Christ's constant presence within us, and of His power resting upon us.

Jesus, the meek and lowly One, calls us to learn from Him the way to God. Let us think on the words we have been reading until our hearts are filled with this thought: My one great need is humility.

And let us believe that whatever He reveals, He also gives; whatever He is, He shares. As the meek and lowly One, He will come and dwell in the heart that longs for Him.

5

Humility in the Disciples of Jesus

'Let him that is chief among you be as he that doth serve.' —LUKE 22: 26

WE HAVE STUDIED humility in the person and teaching of Jesus; now let's look for it in the circle of His chosen companions—the twelve apostles. If, in their lack of humility, the contrast between Christ and human nature appears even more clearly, this contrast will help us appreciate the mighty change Pentecost brought, and show how real our own share can be in Christ's victory over the pride Satan breathed into humanity.

In the passages already quoted from Jesus' teaching, we have seen the occasions on which the disciples showed how entirely they lacked the grace of humility. Once, they had argued on the road about which of them should be the greatest. Another time, the sons of Zebedee, with their mother, asked for the places of highest honor—seats at Jesus' right and left hand. Later still, at the Last Supper, there was again a dispute over who should be considered the greatest.

It is not that they never humbled themselves.

There were indeed moments when they did. Peter cried out, "Depart from me, Lord, for I am a sinful man." The disciples fell down and worshipped Jesus when He stilled the storm. But these occasional moments only throw into stronger contrast what the usual attitude of their hearts was, as shown in the spontaneous way self revealed itself in other moments.

Studying this contrast in them teaches us important lessons.

First, we see how much faithful and active religion there can be while humility is still painfully lacking.

Look at the disciples. They were passionately devoted to Jesus. They had left everything for Him. The Father had revealed to them that He was the Christ. They believed in Him, loved Him, obeyed His commands. When others turned back, they stayed with Him. They were ready to die with Him. Yet beneath all this lay a dark power—something they barely sensed—something that had to be slain and cast out before they could become true witnesses of Jesus' saving power.

It is still the same today. We may find ministers, evangelists, missionaries, teachers—people in whom the gifts of the Spirit are evident, people through whom multitudes are blessed—and yet, when the testing moment comes, or when closer contact reveals more, the abiding grace of humility can be almost entirely absent.

This only confirms the lesson: humility is one of the first and highest of all graces; one of the most difficult to obtain; one to which our main efforts ought to be directed; one that comes only in power when the fullness of the Spirit makes us sharers of Christ's indwelling life so that He Himself lives within us.

Second, we see how powerless all outward teaching and all personal effort are to conquer pride or produce a humble heart.

For three years the disciples had been in Jesus' training school. He had told them plainly what the main lesson was that He wanted them to learn: "Learn from Me, for I am meek and lowly in heart." Again and again, He spoke to them, to the Pharisees, and to the crowds about humility as the only path to God's glory.

He not only lived before them as the Lamb of God in divine humility, but He also revealed to them the secret of His own life: "The Son of Man came not to be served, but to serve," and, "I am among you as one who serves." He had washed their feet, telling them to follow His example. Yet none of this had truly changed them. Even at the Last Supper, they were still arguing about who was greatest.

No doubt they had often tried to learn His lesson and sincerely resolved not to fail again. But it was useless. Their struggle teaches us a necessary truth: no outward instruction, not even Christ's; no argument, however clear; no admiration for humility, however deep; no resolve or effort, however earnest—none of this can cast out the pride that grips the human heart. When Satan seems to cast out Satan, the result is only a subtler

Humility

and stronger pride returning in disguise.

Only one thing can help: the new nature—Christ's own divine humility—must be revealed in power to take the place of the old nature. It must become as truly our nature as pride once was.

Third, it is only through Christ living within us—in His own divine humility—that we can become truly humble.

Our pride comes from someone else—from Adam; therefore our humility must come from Someone else as well.

Pride feels natural to us and rules with such terrible power because it is part of our very nature. Humility must become ours in the same way: it must become our very self, our true nature. Just as it once felt natural and easy to be proud, it must one day feel natural and easy to be humble. The promise is, 'Where,' even in the heart, 'sin abounded, grace did abound more exceedingly.'

All of Christ's teaching, and the disciples' many failed attempts to obey it, were necessary preparation for the moment when He would enter them with divine power and become within them what He had taught them to want and seek.

In His death, He broke the devil's power, removed sin, and achieved an eternal redemption.

In His resurrection, He received from the Father an entirely new life—the life of humanity filled with the power of God, a life capable of being shared with us, entering our being, renewing us, and filling us with divine power.

In His ascension, He received the Spirit of the Father so that He could do what He could not do while still on earth: make Himself one with those He loved, actually live their life within them, so that they could stand before the Father in a humility like His —because it was His own humility now living and breathing in them.

Then, at Pentecost, He came and took full possession. Everything His teaching had prepared them for—their conviction of sin, their awakening desire and hope—was brought to completion by the mighty change Pentecost brought. And the lives and writings of James, Peter, and John show clearly that everything was different now: the spirit of the humble meek and suffering Jesus truly lived in them.

What should we say to all this? Among those reading these words, there will certainly be different kinds of people.

Some may never have thought deeply about humility before, and may not yet grasp how immensely important it is—how central it is to the life of the Church and every believer.

Others may feel deeply convicted of their lack of humility and have tried earnestly to overcome it, only to fail and grow discouraged.

Still others may be able to testify to real spiritual blessing and power in their lives, and yet they have never faced the uncomfortable truth that those around them still detect an absence of humility.

And finally, some may be able to testify that God has granted them real progress and victory in this grace, even while teaching them how much more they need and may still receive from the fullness of Christ.

Whichever group we belong to, we must recognise how urgently we need a deeper conviction of humility's unique place in the way of Christ—and a deeper conviction of the utter impossibility of the Church or the believer becoming what Christ intends without His humility being acknowledged as His highest glory, His foremost command, and our greatest blessing.

Consider how far the disciples had progressed even while this grace was still terribly lacking in them. Then pray that other gifts may not satisfy us so much that we miss the truth: the absence of humility is the real reason God's power is hindered among us.

Only when we, like the Son, truly know and show that we can do nothing of ourselves, will God freely do all.

It is when the reality of Christ living within us takes its rightful place in the life experience of believers that the Church will clothe herself with her beautiful garments, and humility will then be seen in her teachers and members as the beauty of holiness.

6
Humility in Daily Life

'He that loveth not his brother whom he hath seen, how can he love God whom he hath not seen?'— 1 John 4:20

WHAT A SERIOUS TRUTH this is: our love for God is tested and measured by the way we treat the people around us. If our everyday interactions don't show love, then our supposed love for God is only a delusion.

The same is true of humility. It is easy to imagine that we humble ourselves before God. But humility toward people is the only real evidence that our humility before God is genuine.

Only when humility becomes the natural spirit of our life—something that has made its home within us—will it show itself toward others, just as it did in Christ, who "made Himself of no reputation."

When lowliness of heart is not just a posture or feeling we express in prayer, but a settled way of being, it will quietly shape all our relationships. This is a really important lesson: the humility that truly belongs to us is not what we display in devout moments before God, but is what we carry into the unnoticed moments of every day.

The small, insignificant details of daily life

become the great tests of eternity, because they reveal the spirit that truly rules us. It is in our unguarded moments that our real selves appear. If you want to know whether someone is truly humble, you must watch how they move through the normal ordinary events of the day.

This is exactly how Jesus taught humility. He spoke of it when the disciples were arguing about who was greatest. He pointed it out when He noticed how the Pharisees chose the places of honour. He acted it out when He washed the disciples' feet. His message was unmistakable: humility before God means nothing if it is not proved in humility toward people.

Paul taught the same truth. He urged believers to honour one another, to avoid pride, to think of the lowly, and never to be wise in their own eyes.

To the Romans He writes: 'In honour preferring one another'; 'Set not your mind on high things, but condescend to those that are lowly.' 'Be not wise in your own conceit.'

He wrote to the Corinthians: of love—love that cannot exist without humility—love that does not boast, is not puffed up, and does not seek its own way.

He reminded the Galatians that love makes us servants of one another. He warned them not to chase empty glory or irritate and envy each other. 'Through love be servants one of another. Let us not be desirous of vainglory, provoking one another, envying one another.'

And after describing the riches of the heavenly

life in three wonderful chapters to the Ephesians, he immediately called them to walk in all lowliness and meekness, bearing with one another in love, submitting to one another in reverence for Christ.: 'Therefore, walk with all lowliness and meekness, with long-suffering, forbearing one another in love'; 'Giving thanks always, subjecting yourselves one to another in the fear of Christ.'

To the Philippians he wrote that nothing should be done from pride, but in lowliness of mind each should consider others better than themselves. He pointed them to Christ, who emptied Himself and became a servant.

'Doing nothing through faction or vainglory, but in lowliness of mind, each counting other better than himself. Have the mind in you which was also in Christ Jesus, who emptied Himself, taking the form of a servant, and humbled Himself.'

And to the Colossians, Paul said to clothe themselves with compassion, kindness, humility, meekness, and patience, forgiving each other just as the Lord had forgiven them.

'Put on a heart of compassion, kindness, humility, meekness, long-suffering, forebearing one another, and forgiving each other, even as the Lord forgave you.'

All this teaches us that humility is seen most clearly in our relationships, in how we treat one another.

Humility before God has no value unless it prepares us to show the humility of Jesus in our dealings with people.

Let us, then, study humility in daily life in the light of these words.

The humble person tries, at all times, to live by this rule: 'In honor preferring one another; Servants one of another; Each counting others better than himself; Subjecting yourselves one to another.'

People often ask how we can possibly think of others as better than ourselves when it seems that, in wisdom or holiness or natural or spiritual gifting, many we serve fall far below us. But the very question shows how little we understand true humility.

Real lowliness of heart comes only when, in the light of God, we finally see that we are nothing on our own. It comes when we willingly let go of self—its claims, its comparisons, its demands—and allow God to be everything.

When the soul reaches that place and can truly say, "In losing myself, I have found You," it no longer compares itself with anyone. Self has been surrendered in the presence of God. And so, when it meets others, it does so as one who seeks nothing for himself, as one who is God's servant—and therefore the servant of all.

A faithful servant may indeed be wiser than his master, and yet remain fully a servant. So the humble person looks at every child of God—even the weakest, even the least impressive—and honours them as royalty, for they belong to the King. The spirit of the One who washed His disciples' feet makes it a joy for us to take the lowest place, to gladly become servants to one another.

The humble man knows no jealousy or envy. He can rejoice when others are honored and blessed above himself. He can listen while others are praised and he is forgotten, because in God's presence he has learned to say with Paul, "I am nothing."

He has received the spirit of Jesus—the One who did not please Himself and did not seek His own glory—and that spirit has become the very life within him and principle of his life.

The humble person is always trying to live by this rule: "Honor one another above yourselves; be servants of one another; count others better than yourselves; submit to one another."

In the moments that tempt us most—moments of irritation, impatience, sharp thoughts, or quick words—moments stirred up by the faults and sins of other believers, the humble person quietly remembers and lives out the command: 'Forbearing one another, and forgiving one another, even as the Lord forgave you.'

The humble person has learned that when he put on the Lord Jesus, he also put on the Lord's own heart: compassion, kindness, humility, meekness, gentleness, and patience.

Jesus has taken the place of self. And because of that, it is no longer impossible to forgive as Jesus forgave.

His humility is not merely a collection of modest phrases or self-deprecating thoughts. It is, as Paul wrote, a heart of humility—wrapped in compassion and kindness, gentleness and patience— the quiet, tender spirit recognised everywhere as the mark of the Lamb of God.

In striving after the higher experiences of the Christian life, the believer is often in danger of aiming at and rejoicing in what one might call the more human virtues, —courage, joy, contempt of the world, zeal, self-sacrifice. Even the old Stoic philosophers admired and practised these.

But the gentler, deeper, more heavenly graces—the ones Jesus brought from heaven and lived out before us—are often hardly valued at all or thought about: poverty of spirit, meekness, humility, lowliness of heart.

These are the graces most closely tied to His cross, to the death of self.

Therefore, let us put on a heart of compassion, kindness, humility, gentleness, patience. Let us prove and demonstrate our Christlikeness not only in our zeal for the lost, but most of all in how we treat our brothers and sisters—by being patient with them and forgiving them, even as the Lord forgave us.

Study carefully the Bible's portrait of the humble person. Then ask our fellow Christians—and even the watching world—whether they see that likeness in us.

Don't be satisfied with anything less than taking each of these Scriptures as God's promise of what He intends to work in you; as the written revelation of what the Spirit of Jesus will birth within us if we but let him.

And whenever we see our own failures or weakness, let it simply drive us back—humbly and gently—to the meek and lowly Lamb of God. For wherever He is truly enthroned in the heart, His humility and gentleness will flow out of our lives like living water.

Once more, I must repeat what I have said before: we scarcely realise how much the Church suffers because of the absence of true humility—the blessed "nothingness" that makes room for God's power to work and be proved as God's.

Not long ago, a Christian friend, well acquainted with various mission bases, shared his deep grief at seeing how often the spirit of love and patience was missing among missionaries. People who in Europe could choose companions suited to their temperament were now living and working side by side with those whose personalities clashed with theirs. And instead of bearing with each other, loving, and keeping the unity of the Spirit, they grew weary and hindered one another. All because humility—the kind that counts itself nothing, delights to be the least, and seeks only to serve and comfort others—was lacking among them.

How is it that those who have gladly given up their lives for Christ find it so difficult to give themselves up for their brothers and sisters? Isn't the fault partly with the Church? We have spoken too little of Christ's humility as the first character virtue, the greatest fruit, the greatest grace, the very heart of His Spirit. We have seldom shown, by teaching or example, how essential and how attainable this Christlike humility truly is.

But we must not lose heart. The discovery of our

Humility

lack should only stir us to greater expectation from God. Let us see every difficult brother or sister as God's instrument of grace—His way of purifying us and shaping us into the humility of Jesus through His life flowing through us.

Let us trust so fully in God's all-sufficiency, in the All of God, and the nothing of self, and that as seeing ourselves as so utterly nothing in our own eyes, that we may, in God's power, only seek to serve one another in love.

Note: I knew Jesus, and He was very precious to my soul: but I found something in me that would not keep sweet and patient and kind. I did what I could to keep it down, but it was there. I besought Jesus to do something for me, and when I gave Him my will, He came to my heart, and took out all that would not be sweet, all that would not be kind, all that would not be patient, and then He shut the door.'

—GEORGE FOXE.

7
Humility and Holiness

"Which say, Stand by thyself; for I am holier than thou." — ISAIAH 65:5.

WE SPEAK OFTEN about the Holiness movement in our day, and we rightly thank God for it. We hear much about people seeking holiness, claiming holiness, teaching holiness, and gathering in holiness meetings. The wonderful truths of holiness in Christ, and holiness through faith, are being emphasized as never before.

But the great test of whether the holiness we say we desire—or believe we have found—is real and living will be this: Does it produce increasing humility?

Humility is the one essential thing that allows us as God's creatures to have His holiness live within us and shine through us. In Jesus—the Holy One of God, the One who makes us holy—divine humility was the very secret of His life, His death, and His exaltation.

And so the single, unmistakable proof of our holiness will be the humility before both God and people that marks our lives. Humility is the fragrance and the beauty of holiness.

The chief mark of counterfeit holiness is its lack

of humility. Every seeker after holiness must be on guard, lest unconsciously something begun in the Spirit ends up being completed in the flesh, and pride slips in where we least expect it.

Two men went up into the temple to pray: one a Pharisee, the other a tax collector. There is no place so sacred that the Pharisee cannot enter it. Pride can raise its head even in the temple of God and turn worship itself into a platform for self-exaltation.

Since Christ exposed this danger so plainly, the Pharisee has learned to disguise himself as the publican. And so both the person who confesses deep sinfulness and the one who claims high holiness must stay alert.

When we most desire our heart to become God's temple, we may find the two men rising up within us to pray. And the publican part must learn that his danger is not the Pharisee beside him who despises him, but the Pharisee within, who praises and exalts him.

In the temple of God, when we believe ourselves nearest His holiness, we must beware of pride. 'Now there was a day when the sons of God came to present themselves before the Lord, and Satan came also among them.'

"God, I thank You that I am not like other men, or even like this tax collector." It is often precisely in that which is a legitimate reason for thanksgiving, even in the very thanksgiving we offer to God, that self finds a way to congratulate itself. Even when our lips speak the language of penitence and trust in God's mercy alone, the Pharisee may echo our words and turn them into self-approval. Pride can wrap itself in the garments of praise or penitence alike.

The words "I am not like other men" may be rejected and condemned, yet the spirit beneath them often lingers—especially in what we feel or say about fellow believers. If you want to know whether this is true, just listen to how churches and Christians often speak of each other. How little of the meekness and gentleness of Jesus we see. How rarely we remember that deep humility should be the keynote of how the servants of Jesus speak of themselves and each other.

Are there not many churches, gatherings of believers, missions, conventions, committees, and even mission bases far from home, where harmony has been broken and God's work hindered because people who are considered godly have shown, through touchiness, haste, impatience, self-defence, self-assertion, sharp judgments, and unkind words, that they did not consider others better than themselves? Their holiness has had very little of the meekness of the saints.

In the spiritual lives of many, there may have been moments of deep humbling and brokenness. But how different such moments are from being clothed with humility, from possessing an actual humble spirit, from having the lowliness of mind that counts oneself the servant of others, and so reflects the very mind that was in Christ Jesus.

'Stand by; for I am holier than thou!' What a satire on holiness. Jesus—the Holy One—is the humble One. The holiest people will always be the most humble. There is no holiness except God's holiness; whatever holiness we possess is simply the measure of how much of God's life is in us.

And the more of God we have, the deeper our humility will be, because humility is nothing more than the fading away of self in the clear sight that God is everything. The holiest will always be the humblest.

Sadly, even though the bold, boastful spirit of the Jew in Isaiah's time is rarely found today—our manners would hardly allow such open pride—the same attitude often appears in more subtle forms. It shows itself in the way Christians treat one another, and in the way they regard people of the world. It appears in the tone in which opinions are offered, in the spirit with which work is undertaken, and in the eagerness with which faults are exposed.

The outward behaviour may resemble that of the penitent publican, but the voice underneath is still that of the Pharisee: "God, I thank You that I am not like other men."

And is there really such a thing as true humility, where people honestly count themselves "less than the least of all saints" and gladly take the place of a servant to all? Yes, there is. "Love does not boast, is not puffed up, seeks not its own." Where the Spirit of divine love is poured into the heart—where Christ, the meek and lowly Lamb of God, is truly formed within—a new power appears. It is the power of a perfect love that forgets self and finds joy in blessing others, in bearing with them, in honoring them, no matter how weak or unworthy they may be.

Where this love enters, God Himself enters. And when God reveals Himself as All, the creature naturally becomes nothing. And when a person becomes nothing before God, they cannot be anything but humble toward their fellow-creatures. The presence of God becomes not an occasional feeling, but a covering under which the soul continually lives. Deep humility before God becomes the sanctuary from which all words and actions flow.

May God teach us that our thoughts, words, and attitudes toward other people are the real test of our humility before Him. And may we learn that our humility before Him is the only power that can make us truly humble toward others. Our humility must be nothing less than the life of Christ—the Lamb of God—alive within us.

Let all teachers of holiness, whether in the pulpit or on the stage, and all seekers after holiness, whether in the closet or the convention, take warning. There is no pride so dangerous, because none is so subtle and insidious, as the pride that hides inside our pursuit of holiness.

It is not that a person ever openly says, or even consciously thinks, "Stand back; I am holier than you." No, the very thought would be shocking to us. And yet, without noticing it, a quiet habit of soul can form—a sense of satisfaction in our own attainments, an inability to avoid seeing how far we imagine ourselves to be ahead of others.

This spirit shows itself not only in deliberate self-assertion—though sometimes that happens too—but far more often in the simple lack of that deep self-abasement which will always characterise a soul that has truly seen the glory of God (Job 42:5–6; Isa. 6:5).

It reveals itself not only in our words or thoughts, but in our tone—in the way we speak of others. Those who have spiritual discernment can sense the presence of self, even when it is carefully disguised. The world, too, with its sharp eyes, notices it, and points it out as evidence that the profession of a heavenly life does not always produce heavenly fruit.

We must beware. Unless we make it our deliberate aim—with every step forward in what we imagine to be holiness—to grow also in humility, we may find that we have been delighting in beautiful thoughts and stirring feelings, in solemn acts of consecration and faith, while the one sure sign of God's presence—the disappearance of self—was missing all along.

Come, let us flee to Jesus. Let us hide ourselves in Him until we are clothed with His humility. That alone is our holiness.

Note: ME is a very demanding creature. It insists on the best seat and the highest place, and feels deeply wounded if its claims are not recognised. Most quarrels among Christian workers arise from the clamouring of this gigantic ME. Very few of us understand the true secret of taking the lowest place.

—Mrs Smith, *Everyday Religion*

8

Humility and Sin

'Sinners, of whom I am chief.'—1 TIM. 1: 15

HUMILITY IS OFTEN treated as if it were the same as feeling sorry for sin. Because of that, many people assume the only way to grow in humility is to stay constantly focused on sin.

But we have learned, I think, that humility is something deeper and richer. We have seen, in the teaching of Jesus and throughout the New Testament, how often humility is commanded without any direct reference to sin at all.

In its very nature—its place in the relationship between the creature and the Creator—in the life that Jesus lived and now imparts to us, humility is the essence of holiness and the secret of being blessed. Humility is the putting aside of self so that God may be enthroned as all in all. Wherever God is everything, self becomes nothing.

Yet I hardly need to say how deeply man's sin and God's grace intensify the humility of God's people. Look at the Apostle Paul. Throughout his life as a redeemed and holy man, the memory of his former sin remained alive within him.

We know well the passages in which he recalls his

days as a persecutor and blasphemer:

'I am the least of the apostles, that am not worthy to be called an apostle, because I persecuted the Church of God. ...I laboured more abundantly than they all; yet not I, but the grace of God which was with me' (1 Cor. 15. 9,10).

'Unto me, who am less than the least of all saints, was this grace given, to preach to the heathen' (Eph. 3: 8).

'I was before a blasphemer, and a persecutor, and injurious; howbeit I obtained mercy, because I did it ignorantly in unbelief. ...Christ Jesus came into the world to save sinners, of whom I am chief' (1 Tim. 1:13, 15).

God's grace had saved him. God remembered his sins no more. But Paul could never forget how terribly he had sinned. The more he rejoiced in God's salvation, and the more deeply he tasted God's grace, the clearer his awareness became that he was a sinner who had been saved—and that salvation had meaning only because he knew himself to be such a sinner.

Never could Paul forget that it was a sinner whom God had taken into His arms and crowned with His love.

The passages we just quoted are often used as if Paul were admitting to sinning every day. But a careful reading in context shows that this is not what he is saying.

The passages' meaning is far deeper. The words point to something that lasts for all eternity—the sense of awe, adoration and worship that will fill the humility of the redeemed as they bow before the throne, knowing they were washed from their sins by the blood of the Lamb.

Even in glory, they can never cease to be ransomed sinners; and in this life, God's child can never stand in the full light of His love without recognizing that the sin from which he was saved is the only basis for all that grace has promised to give.

The humility with which a person first comes to God as a sinner takes on a new meaning when he discovers that humility also belongs to him simply as a creature. And then, in return, the humility that belongs to him as a creature gains its deepest and richest notes of worship when the creature remembers what it means to be a living testimony to God's astonishing redeeming love.

The real significance of Paul's words becomes even clearer when we notice something remarkable: throughout his entire Christian life, even in the letters where he opens his heart most personally, he never once offers anything like a confession of sin. He never speaks of failure or deficiency, never hints to his readers that he has neglected a duty or acted against the law of perfect love.

On the contrary, there are more than a few passages in which he vindicates himself in language that means nothing if it does not appeal to a faultless life before God and men.

'Ye are witnesses, and God also, how holily, and righteously, and unblameably we behaved ourselves toward you' (1 Thess. 2 10). 'Our glorying is this, the testimony of our conscience, that in holiness and sincerity of God we behaved ourselves in the world, and more abundantly to you ward' (2 Cor. 1. 12).

This is not an ideal he is reaching for, nor a hope he holds out—it is an appeal to what his actual life had been. Whatever explanation we give for this absence of any confession of sin, everyone must agree that it points to a life lived in the power of the Holy Spirit, a life rarely seen or even expected in our own day.

The point I want to stress is this: the very fact that Paul never speaks of ongoing sin only strengthens the truth that deeper humility does not come from daily sinning.

Instead, it comes from a constant, never-forgotten awareness—made all the clearer by abundant grace—that our only true place before God, our one place of blessing, is to stand as people whose greatest joy is to confess that we are sinners saved by grace.

With Paul's deep awareness of how terribly he had once sinned—before grace reached him—and with his present consciousness of being kept from sin by that same grace, he still lived with a constant sense of the dark, hidden power of sin that was always waiting to re-enter his life. It was a power held back only by the presence and strength of Christ living within him.

'In me, that is, in my flesh, dwelleth no good thing;'—these words in Romans 7 describe what the flesh remains right to the end of life. The glorious freedom of Romans 8—'The law of the Spirit of life in Christ Jesus hath now made me free from the law of sin, which once led me captive—does not mean the flesh has been destroyed or made holy. Rather, it means a continual victory is given by the Spirit as He keeps putting to death the deeds of the body.

As health drives out disease, as light swallows up darkness, as life overcomes death, so Christ's indwelling presence through the Spirit becomes the health, the light, and the life of the soul.

Yet with this victory comes a humble awareness of helplessness and danger—an awareness that gently steadies our faith. It produces a sober, steady sense of dependence—one in which even the highest faith and deepest joy serve a humility that survives only by the grace of God.

The three passages above all show that it was the astonishing grace poured out upon Paul—and his awareness that he needed that grace every moment—that humbled him so deeply.

The grace of God that worked with him and enabled him to labor more than all the rest; the grace that commissioned him to proclaim to the nations the unsearchable riches of Christ; the grace that overflowed toward him with faith and love in Christ Jesus—this grace, whose very nature and glory is to meet sinners, kept alive in him the vivid sense of having once sinned and of being always liable to sin.

'Where sin abounded, grace did abound more exceedingly.'

This reveals that the essence of grace is to confront sin and take it away; and that the greater our experience of grace, the more intense our awareness of being sinners must become. It is not sin itself, but God's grace—showing a person, and continually reminding him, what a sinner he was—that keeps him truly humble.

It is not sin, but grace, that makes me honestly recognize myself as a sinner, and makes the sinner's place of deep self-abasement the only place I never leave.

I fear that there are many who, with strong expressions of self-condemnation and self-reproach, have tried to humble themselves, only to admit with sorrow that a humble spirit—a true "heart of humility," together with kindness, compassion, meekness, and patience—is still as distant as ever from them.

Being occupied with oneself, even in the deepest self-loathing, can never free us from self. It is God's revelation—not only through the law that exposes sin but through His grace that delivers from it—that makes us humble.

The law may break the heart with fear; only grace can create that sweet humility that becomes a joy to the soul and its second nature.

It was the revelation of God in His holiness drawing near in grace that caused Abraham and Jacob, Job and Isaiah, to bow so low. It is the soul that waits for, trusts, and worships God—the Creator as the All in a creature's nothingness, the Redeemer as the All for a sinner in his sinfulness—that finds itself so filled with God's presence that there is no room left for self.

Only then can the promise be fulfilled: 'The

haughtiness of man shall be brought low, and the Lord alone be exalted in that day.'

It is the sinner who lives in the full light of God's holy, redeeming love—in the experience of the divine love that dwells within us through Christ and the Holy Spirit—who cannot help but be humble.

Deliverance from self comes by being occupied with God, not by being occupied with sin.

9
Humility and Faith

'How can ye believe, which receive glory from one another, and the glory that cometh from the only God ye seek not?' JOHN 5: 44.

IN AN ADDRESS I recently heard, the speaker said that the blessings of the deeper Christian life are often like objects set behind a shop window. We can see them clearly, but we cannot reach them. If someone told a man to stretch out his hand and take them, he would reply that he cannot —because a thick pane of glass stands between him and what he wants

In the same way, Christians may see the beautiful promises of perfect peace and rest, of love and joy overflowing, of steady communion with God and a life full of fruit. Yet they still feel that something stands between them and the actual enjoyment of these gifts.

And what is that barrier?

Nothing but pride.

The promises given to faith are wonderfully free and certain. The invitations of Scripture are strong and urgent. The mighty power of God, on which faith may rely, is always near. So if the blessings do not become ours, the obstacle cannot be in the promises themselves—it must be in something that hinders faith.

Jesus tells us clearly what that something is: pride. "How can you believe," He says, "when you receive glory from one another?"

When we see how pride and faith oppose each other at the deepest level, we realise that humility and faith are inseparable. We can never have more genuine faith than we have real humility.

A person may have strong intellectual conviction. He may firmly believe the doctrines of Scripture. But if pride still rules in the heart, then the living faith that lays hold of God and moves His hand becomes impossible.

Faith asks us to pause and consider what it really is. At its core, faith is the confession of our own nothingness and helplessness. It is the surrender that waits for God to act. It is, by its very nature, the most humbling posture we can take—accepting that we are entirely dependent, able to claim or do nothing except what grace freely gives.

True humility is the attitude that prepares the soul to live entirely by trust. Every subtle stirring of pride—whether in self-seeking, self-will, self-confidence, or self-exaltation—strengthens that self which cannot enter the kingdom. It cannot receive the things of the kingdom because it refuses to let God be what He must be there: the All in All.

Faith is the spiritual organ of the body or spiritual sense by which we perceive and receive the realities of the heavenly world. It seeks the glory that comes from God alone—the glory that appears only where

God is everything. But as long as we take glory from one another, as long as we seek and cherish and guard the honor and reputation that come from men, we cannot seek or receive the glory that comes from God.

Pride makes faith impossible. Salvation comes through a cross and a crucified Christ. Salvation is fellowship with the crucified One, sharing the spirit of His cross. Salvation is union with the humility of Jesus—finding delight in it, and receiving it as our own.

Is it any wonder, then, that our faith is so weak? Pride still rules so much of our lives, and we have scarcely begun to desire or ask for humility as the most necessary and most blessed part of salvation.

Humility and faith are more closely connected in Scripture than many realize. We can see this in the life of Christ. There are two occasions where He spoke of someone having great faith.

The centurion—whose faith made Jesus marvel, and of whom He said, 'I have not found so great faith, no, not in Israel!' —first declared, 'I am not worthy that Thou shouldst come under my roof'?
The mother, to whom Jesus said, '"O woman, great is thy faith!' , accepted being called a dog and replied, '"Yea, Lord, yet the dogs eat of the crumbs'?

It is humility that brings a soul to nothing before God. It removes every hindrance to faith and makes the heart fear only one thing—that it should dishonor God by failing to trust Him completely.

Isn't the true cause of our failure in pursuing

holiness our lack of humility?

We had no idea to what an extent pride and self were still secretly working within us, and how alone God by His incoming and His mighty power could cast them out.

We did not understand how deeply self must be cast out, and how only God's incoming power could do it.

We did not realize that the new divine nature must entirely replace the old self before we could truly be humble.

We did not see that absolute, constant, all-pervading humility must be the root posture of every prayer, every approach to God, and every interaction with people.

We did not see that without this humility, we might as well try to see without eyes or live without breath.

We cannot believe, or draw near to God, or remain in His love without being humble and possessing a heart saturated with lowliness.

Brother, have we not made a mistake in trying so hard to believe, while the old proud self was still trying to grasp God's gifts for its own possession?

No wonder we could not believe.

Let us take another path.

Let us seek first to humble ourselves under God's mighty hand—He will lift us up.

The cross, the death, and the grave into which Jesus descended were His path to God's glory.

They are our path as well.

Let this be our one desire and fervent prayer: to

be humbled with Him and like Him. Let us welcome anything that humbles us before God or people— for this alone is the road that leads into the glory of God.

You may feel inclined to ask a question. I have spoken of some who enjoy blessed spiritual experiences, or who become instruments of blessing to others, and yet still lack humility. You ask whether their usefulness does not prove that they possess real —perhaps even strong—faith, despite clearly seeking too much of the honor that comes from people.

More than one answer could be given. But the answer most relevant here is this: yes, they do possess a measure of faith, and in proportion to that faith— and the gifts God has given them—is the blessing they bring to others.

Yet even in that blessing, the full working of their faith is hindered by the lack of humility. The blessing that flows through them is often shallow or short-lived precisely because they are not the "nothing" that opens the way for God to be "all." A deeper humility would, without question, produce a deeper and more lasting blessing.

If the Holy Spirit were not only working in them with power, but dwelling in them in the fullness of His grace—especially His humility—He would, through them, impart Himself to new believers in a way that brings lasting power, holiness, and stability, which we now see far too little of.

"How can you believe, when you receive glory from one another?" Brother, nothing can cure the desire for human praise—or the hurt, anger, and sensitivity that rise when it is withheld—except this: giving yourself wholly to seek only the glory that comes from God.

Let the glory of the All-glorious God be everything to you. Then you will be freed from the glory of men and the glory of self, and you will rejoice to be nothing.

And from this "nothingness," your faith will grow strong, giving glory to God. You will find that the deeper you sink in humility before Him, the nearer He comes to fulfilling every desire of your faith.

10
Humility and Death to Self

'He humbled Himself and became obedient unto death.'—PHIL.2: 8.

HUMILITY IS THE PATH that leads to death, because in death it gives the highest possible proof of its perfection. Humility is the blossom; death to self is the fully ripened fruit. Jesus humbled Himself to the point of death and opened the path in which we too must walk.

There was no other way for Jesus to show His complete surrender to God, or for to rise out of our human nature into the glory of the Father, except through death. And so it is for us. Humility must lead us into death to self, so that we demonstrate how completely we have yielded ourselves to humility and to God.

Only then are we freed from our fallen nature, and find the road into life in God—the road into the full birth of the new nature, where humility becomes our breath and our joy.

We have already spoken of what Jesus did for His disciples when He shared His resurrection life with them—when, through the coming of the Holy Spirit, He Himself, the glorified and enthroned embodiment of meekness, descended from heaven to dwell within them.

He gained the power to do this through death. The life He imparted was, at its core, a life that had passed through death. It was a life surrendered to death and gained through death. He who came to live within them was One who had been dead and now lives forever.

His life, His presence, His very person, carries the signs of death—signs of a life born out of death. And that life in His disciples carries those signs as well. It is only as the Spirit of the crucified and dying Christ dwells and works within the soul that the power of His life can truly be known.

The first and greatest sign of the dying of the Lord Jesus—the chief death-sign of a true follower of Christ—is humility.

This is true for two reasons: only humility leads to perfect death, and only death perfects humility. The two are, by their very nature, one. Humility is the bud; death is the fruit brought to full perfection.

Humility leads to perfect death.
Humility means giving up self and taking the place of complete nothingness before God.

Jesus humbled Himself and became obedient even to death.

In dying, He gave the highest proof that He had surrendered His will entirely to God.

In death He yielded His self, with its natural shrinking from the cup. He gave up the life He shared with our human nature.

He died to self and to the sin that tempted Him. In doing so, as man, He entered into the perfect life of God.

Without His boundless humility—counting Himself nothing except a servant to do and suffer God's will—He never would have died.

This gives us the answer to a question so often asked, but rarely understood: How can I die to self?

The death to self is not your work—it is God's work. In Christ, you are dead to sin; the life in you has already passed through death and resurrection. You may be sure that you truly are dead to sin. But the full expression of this death in your attitude and conduct depends on how fully the Holy Spirit imparts the power of Christ's death to you.

Here is where the real instruction comes in: if you want to enter into full fellowship with Christ in His death, and know full deliverance from self, humble yourself. This is your one duty. Place yourself before God in utter helplessness. Agree wholeheartedly with the truth that you cannot kill or revive yourself. Sink down into your nothingness with a meek, patient, trusting surrender to God.

Accept every humiliation. Look at every person who irritates or tries you as a means of grace to make you spiritually mature—God's tool to humble you. Use every opportunity to humble yourself before others as a way of staying humble before God. He will accept this self-humbling as the proof that your whole heart desires it. He will receive it as the best prayer you could offer. He will see it as the preparation for His own mighty work—when, by the strengthening of His Spirit, He reveals Christ fully in you, forming Him in you as the true Servant who dwells within your heart.

It is the path of humility that leads to perfect death—the full and complete experience that we are dead in Christ.

Then comes the second truth: only this death leads to perfect humility. Beware of the mistake so many make—wanting to be humble, yet afraid of going "too far." They surround humility with qualifications and boundaries, with endless reasoning about what humility should or shouldn't do, until they never truly yield themselves to it. Beware of this.

Humble yourself to the point of death. It is through death to self that humility reaches its perfection.

Be sure that at the root of every real experience of greater spiritual maturity, of every true advance in consecration, of every genuine increase in Christlikeness, there must be a death to self that proves itself before God and people in our character and habits.

It is sadly possible to speak a lot about the "death-life" and the "Spirit-walk," while even the most loving observer can clearly see how much self remains. Death to self has no surer mark than a humility that makes no name for itself, empties itself out, and takes the form of a servant.

It is possible to talk much, and sincerely, about fellowship with a despised and rejected Christ, and of bearing His cross, while the meek, lowly, gentle humility of the Lamb of God is barely visible—barely even sought.

Humility

The Lamb of God stands for two things: meekness and death.

Let us receive Him in both. In Him they are inseparable; in us they must be as well.

What a hopeless task it would be if we had to do this work ourselves! Our natural self can never conquer our natural self—not even with the help of grace. One's own self can never cast out self, not even in a renewed believer. But thank God, the work has already been done, finished, and perfected forever. The death of Jesus—once and for all—is our death to self. And His ascension, His entrance forever into the Most Holy Place, has given us the Holy Spirit, who now imparts to us, in power, the very reality of that death-life and makes it truly our own.

As the soul follows Jesus in the pursuit and practice of humility, it becomes more aware of its need for something deeper. Desire grows. Hope is stirred. Faith is strengthened. And the soul learns to look up, to claim, and to receive the true fullness of Christ's Spirit—the power that can daily maintain His death to self and sin in living reality, and can make humility the all-pervading spirit of our lives. (See Note C.)

'Are you ignorant that all of us who were baptised into Jesus Christ were baptised into His death? Reckon yourselves to be dead to sin, but alive to God in Christ Jesus. Present yourselves to God as those alive from the dead.'

The whole self-awareness of a Christian must be shaped and saturated by the spirit that filled the death of Christ. At all times the Christian must present himself to God as one who has died in Christ, and who in Christ is now alive from the dead—bearing in his body the dying of the Lord Jesus. His life carries a twofold mark: its roots sink, in true humility, deep into the grave of Jesus—into death to sin and death to self; and its head lifts upward in resurrection power toward the heaven where Jesus is.

Claim by faith the death and the life of Jesus as your own. Enter His grave, where rest from self and all its striving—the rest of God—is found. With Christ, who entrusted His spirit into the Father's hands, humble yourself and descend each day into complete, helpless dependence on God. He will raise you up and exalt you.

Sink every morning into deep, deep nothingness in the grave of Jesus; each day the life of Jesus will be made visible in you.

Let a willing, loving, restful, joyful humility be the unmistakable mark that you have indeed claimed your birthright—the baptism into the death of Christ. "By one offering He has perfected forever those who are sanctified."

Souls that enter into His humiliation will find in Him the power to see and count the self as dead. And, having learned and received this from Him, they will walk with all humility, lowliness and meekness, bearing with one another and being patient in love. The death-life reveals itself in a meekness and lowliness like that of Christ.

11
Humility and Happiness

'Most gladly therefore will I rather glory in my weaknesses, that the strength of Christ may rest upon me. Wherefore I take pleasure in weakness: for when I am weak then am I strong.'—2 COR. 12. 9–10.

SO PAUL DID NOT exalt himself because of the extraordinary greatness of the revelations he had received, a thorn in the flesh was given to him to keep him humble. His first desire was to be rid of it, and he begged the Lord three times to take it away.

The answer came that the trial was actually a gift; that in the weakness and humiliation it caused, the Lord's grace and strength could shine more clearly.

Paul immediately stepped into a new understanding of the trial. Instead of only enduring it, he began to rejoice in it. Instead of seeking escape, he took pleasure in it.

He had discovered that the place that humbles us is the place of blessing, the place of power, and the place of joy.

Every Christian passes through two stages while pursuing humility.

In the first stage, he fears and flees from

everything that can humble him, and he seeks deliverance from it. He has not yet learned to seek humility at any cost. He accepts the command to be humble and tries to obey it, only to discover how completely he fails.

He prays for humility—sometimes very earnestly—but in his secret heart he prays even more, if not in words then in unspoken wishes, to be kept from the very things that would actually make him humble.

He is not yet in love with humility as the beauty of the Lamb of God and the joy of heaven, so he is not ready to "sell all" in order to gain it.

In his pursuit of humility, and even in his prayers for it, there is still a sense of burden and bondage. Humbling himself has not yet become the natural expression of a heart and nature that have truly become humble. It has not yet become his joy and delight. He cannot yet say, "Most gladly do I glory in weakness; I take pleasure in whatever humbles me."

But can we hope to reach a stage where this truly becomes our desire? Yes, absolutely. And what will bring us there? The same thing that brought Paul there—a new revelation of the Lord Jesus.

Nothing but the presence of God can reveal and expel self. Paul was to receive a clearer insight into the deep truth that the presence of Jesus drives out every desire to seek anything in ourselves. His presence teaches us to delight in every humiliation that prepares our hearts for a fuller manifestation and revelation of Him.

Our humiliations, when they lead us into the experience of the presence and power of Jesus, teach us to choose humility as our highest blessing. Let us try to learn the lessons Paul's story teaches us.

We may meet more mature believers, powerful teachers, and people with heavenly experiences who still have not fully learned the lesson of perfect humility—of gladly glorying in weakness. We see this in Paul. The danger of self-exaltation was nearing him. He did not yet fully know what it meant to be nothing— to die so that Christ alone might live in him— or to take pleasure in everything that brought him low.

It seems as if this was the highest lesson he had yet to learn: full conformity to his Lord in that self-emptying where he truly gloried in weakness so that God might be all.

The highest lesson a believer has to learn is humility. Every Christian who seeks to grow in holiness needs to remember this. You may give yourself fully to God, show strong zeal, and have deep spiritual experiences, and yet—unless the Lord works in you in a special way—you can still fall into a quiet, unnoticed pride that mixes itself into all you do.

That is why we must take this lesson to heart: the greatest holiness is the deepest humility. And we must understand that humility does not simply appear on its own. It grows only as the Lord works it into us through His faithful dealings and through our faithful response.

So let us look honestly at our own lives in light of

Paul's experience. Do we truly rejoice in our weaknesses? Do we take pleasure, as Paul did, in hardships, in needs, and in difficulties? Let us ask ourselves whether we have learned to see a rebuke—fair or unfair—a criticism from a friend or an enemy, a wrongdoing, a trouble, or any inconvenience others cause us, as a chance to show that Jesus is everything to us.

These moments reveal whether our own comfort or honour matters to us at all, or whether we truly welcome the humility they bring.

This is a blessed place to reach: the deep, quiet happiness of heaven that comes from being so free from self that whatever is said or done to us hardly touches us. It is swallowed up in one steady thought: Jesus is all.

Let us trust the One who guided Paul to guide us as well.

Paul needed a very specific kind of discipline, along with direct instruction from the Lord, to learn something even more valuable than the "unutterable things" he heard in heaven. He had to learn to rejoice in weakness and lowliness. We need that same lesson—deeply and desperately.

The Lord who cared for Paul will care for us too. He watches over us with a loving and protective jealousy, working constantly "lest we exalt ourselves."

When we do begin to exalt ourselves, He works to show us the danger we are in and to set us free. He uses trials, weakness, and trouble to bring us low. Through these things He teaches us that His grace

Humility

truly is enough.

As we learn this, we begin to see that the very things which humble us are the things we can accept —even welcome. They keep us low before Him. They keep us dependent. They keep us safe.

His strength is made perfect in our weakness. His presence fills the emptiness that humbling experiences create. This becomes the secret of a humility that does not fade.

Like Paul, we can come to a place where we see clearly what God is doing in us and through us, and still say, "I am nothing," without fear or shame.

Paul could boldly declare, "In nothing was I behind the chiefest apostles, though I am nothing." His humiliations—the things that wounded his pride —became the doorway into real humility. And real humility brought with it a strange and wonderful gladness, even a joy in everything that kept him low.

Let us trust the One who guided Paul to guide us as well. Paul needed special discipline, and special instruction, to learn something even more precious than the heavenly revelations he had received—he had to learn what it meant to rejoice in weakness and lowliness. We need the same lesson, and we need it deeply.

God watches us with a loving and jealous care, doing all He can to keep us from exalting ourselves. When pride begins to rise, He works to expose it and free us from it. Through trials, weaknesses, and difficulties, He brings us lower and lower, until we finally learn that His grace is everything. Only then do we begin to take pleasure in the very things that humble us and keep us dependent on Him.

As His strength is made perfect in our weakness, and His presence fills our emptiness, we begin to discover the secret of a humility that does not collapse or fade. Paul could look honestly at all God had done through him and still say, "I am nothing," because his humiliations had led him into true humility. And that humility had become a source of real joy, allowing him to glory in everything that made him low.

"Most gladly will I glory in my weaknesses, so that the power of Christ may rest on me. I take pleasure in weaknesses."

The humble person has learned the secret of lasting gladness. The weaker he feels, the lower he bows, the more clearly he sees his own shortcomings, the more deeply he experiences the power and presence of Christ. And when he says with Paul, "I am nothing," the Lord answers again and again: "My grace is enough for you."

We must keep two truths in mind.

First, the danger of pride is far greater and far closer than we imagine. It is especially dangerous at the very moment of our highest spiritual experiences. The preacher who speaks with power, the teacher on the holiness platform, the Christian sharing a testimony, the evangelist whose work seems to overflow with blessing—all of these stand in a place of hidden danger. Paul was in danger without even realizing it. What Christ did for him is recorded as a warning to us.

Second, the grace for humility is real. If people

have ever said of a preacher or a holiness teacher, "He is full of himself," or "He does not live what he preaches," or "His blessing has not made him gentler or humbler," then let that be said no more. Jesus, whom we trust, is able to make us humble.

Let us trust the One who guided Paul to guide us as well. Paul needed special discipline, along with special teaching, to learn something even more precious than the unspeakable things he saw in heaven—he had to learn what it meant to glory in weakness and lowliness. We need that same lesson, and we need it deeply.

God watches over us with a jealous and loving care, guarding us "lest we exalt ourselves." When pride begins to rise, He works to expose it and free us from it. Through trouble, weakness, and trial, He tries to bring us low until we learn that His grace is everything. Then we can begin to take pleasure in whatever keeps us low.

His strength becomes perfect in our weakness. His presence fills our emptiness. This is the secret of a humility that does not fade.

Like Paul, we can look at all God does in and through us and still say, "I am nothing." His humiliations led him into true humility, which brought the strange gladness, the steady joy, and even the delight in everything that humbled him.

"Most gladly will I glory in my weaknesses, that the power of Christ may rest upon me; wherefore I take pleasure in weaknesses."

The humble person has learned the secret of constant joy. The weaker he feels, the lower he sinks.

The more his humiliations appear, the more fully the power and presence of Christ become his. And when he says, "I am nothing," the voice of his Lord brings deeper joy: "My grace is sufficient for you."

12
Humility and Exaltation

'He that humbleth himself shall be exalted.' —LUKE 14: 11, 18: 13.

'God giveth grace to the humble. Humble yourself in the sight of the Lord, and He shall exalt you.'—JAS. 4: 10.

'Humble yourselves therefore under the mighty hand of God, that He may exalt you in due time.'—1 PET. 5. 6.

"He that humbleth himself shall be exalted." —Luke 14:11; 18:13.

"God gives grace to the humble. Humble yourselves in the sight of the Lord, and He will exalt you." —James 4:10.

"Humble yourselves therefore under the mighty hand of God, that He may exalt you in due time." —1 Peter 5:6.

Just yesterday I was asked, "How am I to conquer this pride?"

The answer is simple. Two things are needed.

1. Do the thing God says is your work: humble yourself.

2. Trust Him to do the thing He says is His work: He will exalt you.

The command is clear: humble yourself. But that command does not mean you must somehow defeat the pride in your nature by your own efforts, or create within yourself the gentleness and lowliness of Jesus. That work belongs to God alone. It is the very essence of the exaltation by which He lifts you into the real likeness of His beloved Son.

What the command does mean is this: take every opportunity to humble yourself before God and before people. Do this in confidence that God's grace is already working in you, and in the assurance that more grace for victory will come. Whenever your conscience shines a light on pride in your heart, respond to it. Even through repeated failure, keep taking your stand beneath this unchanging word: humble yourself.

Receive with gratitude everything God allows— whether it comes from inside you or outside you, from friend or enemy, from nature or from grace— anything that reminds you of your need to be humbled and helps you toward it.

Count humility as the mother of all virtues, your first duty before God, the constant safeguard of your soul. Set your heart on it as the source of all blessing.

The promise is absolutely certain: "He that humbleth himself shall be exalted."

Your part is to do the one thing God commands —humble yourself.

God will do the one thing He has promised—He will exalt you. He will give more grace, and He will lift you up at the right time.

All God's dealings with us follow two stages. First comes the stage of preparation. Command and promise meet with our efforts, our weakness, our failures, our partial progress, and the hope that stirs within us for something better. All of this trains and shapes us for what comes next.

Then comes the stage of fulfilment. Faith receives the promise and enters into what it had so often struggled for in vain. This pattern appears in every part of the Christian life and in the pursuit of every virtue. It is woven into the way God works.

In all matters of salvation, God takes the initiative. Then comes our turn. In our attempts at obedience, we discover our weakness. We learn self-despair. We die to our own ability. Only then are we ready, willingly and knowingly, to receive from God the full outcome of what we first accepted from Him without understanding.

In this way, the God who was the Beginning—before we even knew Him or His purpose—is longed for and welcomed as the End, the One who is truly All in All.

It is the same in our pursuit of humility. To every Christian, the command comes straight from the throne of God: humble yourself.

When we honestly try to obey this command, we quickly make two painful discoveries. First, we find a depth of pride in ourselves we never knew existed—an unwillingness to see ourselves as nothing and to submit completely to God. Second, we discover how powerless we are, even with prayer, to defeat this terrible pride.

Blessed is the person who learns, at this point, to put their hope in God and to keep going. Even while pride still rises up inside, they continue to practise real acts of humility before God and before people.

We know how human nature works: actions form habits, habits shape attitudes, attitudes form the will, and the will becomes character. The same is true in the life of grace. As we repeatedly choose humility, the habits and characteristics of humility grow stronger. And as they grow, God—who works in us both to will and to do—strengthens us by His Spirit. The proud heart that once struggled to bow now receives the "more grace" promised to the humble, and the Spirit of Jesus shapes the new nature until Christ the meek and lowly One truly dwells there.

"Humble yourselves in the sight of the Lord, and He will exalt you."

What does this exaltation look like?

The highest glory a human being can have is simply to be a vessel—someone who receives, enjoys, and displays the glory of God. But we can only do this when we are willing to be nothing so that God may be everything. Just as water always flows to the lowest places, God's presence fills the life that lies low and empty before Him. The lower we go, the more freely His glory flows in.

The exaltation God promises is not an external reward apart from Himself. Everything He gives is simply more of Himself, taking deeper possession of us.

Exaltation is not a prize unrelated to humility. It is the natural result of humility. It is the gift of a deeper, God-given lowliness—a true sharing in the humility of the Lamb—that prepares us to receive the fullness of God.

"He who humbles himself will be exalted."
Jesus Himself proves these words true. And His life guarantees their fulfilment in us.

So let us take His yoke and learn from Him, for He is gentle and lowly in heart. If we will stoop to Him as He has stooped to us, He will stoop to us again. We will find ourselves yoked with Him, not unevenly but in perfect fellowship.

As we enter more deeply into His humility—whether by choosing to humble ourselves or by accepting the humbling that others bring—we can be certain that the Spirit of His exaltation, "the Spirit of God and of glory," will rest upon us.

When God regains His rightful place in us, He will lift us up. If we make His glory our aim by humbling ourselves, He will make our glory His concern—perfecting our humility and breathing into us the very Spirit of His Son.

When the life of God fills us completely, nothing will feel more natural—or more sweet—than being nothing, with no thought of self at all, because our whole being will be taken up with the One who fills everything.

"Most gladly will I boast in my weaknesses, so that the power of Christ may rest upon me."

Brother, isn't this the real reason our consecration and our faith have accomplished so little in our pursuit of holiness? We tried to do the work in our own strength while calling it faith. We sought God mainly for our own comfort and happiness. We even rejoiced—often without realizing it—in our own sense of holiness. We did not understand that humility, steady and Christlike humility, a humility that erases self and shapes all our dealings with God and with others, is the most essential element in the holy life we were longing for.

It is only when God possesses me fully that I truly lose myself. Just as the brightness and glory of sunlight makes the tiny speck floating in its beams look smaller than ever, humility is simply taking our place in God's presence as nothing more than a speck resting in the radiance of His love.

May God teach us to believe that being humble —being nothing before Him—is the highest achievement and the richest blessing of the Christian life. He says, "I dwell in the high and holy place, and with the one who is contrite and humble in spirit." May this be our portion.

> 'Oh, to be emptier, lowlier,
> Mean, unnoticed, and unknown,
> And to God a vessel holier,
> Filled with Christ, and Christ alone!'

NOTE A

From W Law—Spirit of Prayer, Pt. 2. p. 73, Edition of Moreton, Canterbury, 1893:

'All this is to make it known the region of eternity that pride can degrade the highest angels into devils, and humility raise fallen flesh and blood to the thrones of angels. Thus, this is the great end of God raising a new creation out of a fallen kingdom of angels: for this end it stands in its state of war betwixt the fire and pride of fallen angels, and the humility of the Lamb of God, that the last trumpet may sound the great truth through the depths of eternity, that evil can have no beginning but from pride, and no end but from humility. The truth is this: Pride may die in you, or nothing of heaven can live in you. Under the banner of the truth, give yourself up to the meek and humble spirit of the holy Jesus. Humility must sow seed, or there can be no reaping in Heaven. Look not at pride only as an unbecoming temper, nor at humility only as a decent virtue: for the one is death, and the other is life; the one is all hell, the other is all heaven. So much as you have of pride within you, you have of the fallen angels alive in you; so much as you have of true humility, so much you have of the Lamb of God within you. Could you see what every stirring of pride does to your soul, you would beg of everything you meet to tear the viper from you, though with the loss of a hand or an eye. Could you see what a sweet, divine, transforming power there is in humility, how it expels the poison of your nature, and makes room for the Spirit of God to live in you, you would rather wish to be the footstool of all the world than want the smallest degree of it.'

NOTE B

From William Law, *Address to the Clergy*, p. 52.

'We need to know two things:

1. That our salvation consists wholly in being saved from ourselves, or that which we are by nature;

2. That in the whole nature of things nothing could be this salvation or saviour to us but such a humility of God as is beyond all expression. Hence the first unalterable term of the Saviour to fallen man: Except a man denies himself, he cannot be My disciple. Self is the whole evil of fallen nature; self-denial is our capacity of being saved; humility is our saviour. ...Self is the root, the branches, the tree, of all the evil of our fallen state. All the evils of fallen angels and men have their birth in the pride of self. On the other hand, all the virtues of the heavenly life are the virtues of humility. It is humility alone that makes the unpassable gulf between heaven and hell. What is then, or in what lies, the great struggle for eternal life? It all lies in the strife between pride and humility: pride and humility are the two master powers, the two kingdoms in strife for the eternal possession of man. There never was, nor ever will

be, but one humility, and that is the one humility of Christ. Pride and self have the all of man, till man has his all from Christ. He therefore only fights the good fight whose strife is that the self-idolatrous nature which he hath from Adam may be brought to death by the supernatural humility of Christ brought to life in him.'

[I hope that this book of Law on the Holy Spirit may be issued by my publisher in the course of the year—A.M.]

NOTE C

'To die to self, or come from under its power, is not, cannot be done, by any active resistance we can make to it by the powers of nature. The one true way of dying to self is the way of patience, meekness, humility, and resignation to God. This is the truth and perfection of dying to self. ...For if I ask you what the Lamb of God means, must you not tell me that it is and means the perfection of patience, meekness, humility, and resignation to God? Must you not therefore say that a desire and faith of these virtues is an application to Christ, is a giving up yourself to Him and the perfection of faith in Him? And then, because this inclination of your heart to sink down in patience, meekness, humility, and resignation to God, is truly giving up all that you are and all that you have from fallen Adam, it is perfectly leaving all you have to follow Christ; it is your highest act of faith in Him. Christ is nowhere but in these virtues; when they are there, He is in His own kingdom. Let this be the Christ you follow.

'The Spirit of divine love can have no birth in any fallen creature, till it wills and chooses to be dead to all self, in a patient, humble resignation to the power and mercy of God.

'I seek for all my salvation through the merits and

mediation of the meek, humble, patient, suffering Lamb of God, who alone hath power to bring forth the blessed birth of these heavenly virtues in my soul. There is no possibility of salvation but in and by the birth of the meek, humble, patient, resigned Lamb of God in our souls. When the Lamb of God hath brought forth a real birth of His own meekness, humility, and full resignation to God in our souls, then it is the birthday of the Spirit of love in our souls, which, whenever we attain, will feast our souls with such peace and joy in God as will blot out the remembrance of everything that we called peace or joy before.

'This way to God is infallible. This infallibility is grounded in the twofold character of our Saviour:

1. As He is the Lamb of God, a principle of all meekness and humility in the soul;

2. As He is the Light of heaven, and blesses eternal nature, and turns it into a kingdom of heaven,—when we are willing to get rest to our souls in meek, humble resignation to God, then it is that He, as the Light of God and heaven, joyfully breaks in upon us, turns our darkness into light, and begins that kingdom of God and of love within us, which will never have an end.'— See *Wholly For God*, pp 84-102.

[Note: The whole passage deserves careful study, showing most remarkably how the continual sinking down in humility before God is, from man's side, the only way to die to self.

[Note: The whole dialogue has been published separately under the title *Dying to Self: A Golden Dialogue*. By William Law. With Notes by A.M. (Nisbet & Co.)

Every one who would study and practise humility will find in this golden dialogue what it is that hinders our humility, how we are to be delivered from it, and what the blessing of the Spirit of Love is that comes to the humble from Christ, the meek and lowly Lamb of God.]

Note D

A Secret of Secrets:
Humility as the Heart of True Prayer

From William Law, *The Spirit of Prayer*, Pt. 2. p. 121.

'Till the spirit of the heart be renewed, till it is emptied of all earthly desires, and stands in an habitual hunger and thirst after God, which is the true spirit of prayer; till then, all our prayer will be, more or less, but too much like lessons given to scholars; and we shall mostly say them, only because we dare not neglect them. But be not discouraged; take the following advice, and then you may go to church without any danger of mere lip-labor or hypocrisy, although there should be a hymn or a prayer, whose language is higher than that of your heart. Do this: go to the church as the publican went to the temple; stand inwardly in the spirit of your mind in that form which he outwardly expressed, when he cast down his eyes, and could only say, 'God be merciful to me, a sinner.' Stand unchangeably, at least in your desire, in this form or state of heart; it will sanctify every petition that comes out of your mouth; and when anything is read or sung or prayed, that is more exalted than your heart is, if you make this an occasion of further sinking down in the spirit of the publican, you will then be helped, and highly blessed, by those prayers and praises which seem only to belong to a heart better than yours.

This, my friend, is a secret of secrets; it will help you to reap where you have not sown, and be a continual source of grace in your soul; for everything that inwardly stirs in you, or outwardly happens to you, becomes a real good to you, if it finds or excites in you this humble state of mind. For nothing is in vain, or without profit to the humble soul; it stands always in a state of divine growth; everything that falls upon it is like a dew of heaven to it. Shut up yourself, therefore, in this form of Humility; all good is enclosed in it; it is a water of heaven, that turns the fire of the fallen soul into the meekness of the divine life, and creates that oil, out of which the love to God and man gets its flame. Be enclosed, therefore, always in it; let it be as a garment wherewith you are always covered, and a girdle with which you are girt; breathe nothing but in and from its spirit; see nothing but with its eyes; hear nothing but with its ears. And then, whether you are in the church or out of the church, hearing the praises of God or receiving wrongs from men and the world, all will be edification, and everything will help forward your growth in the life of God.

A PRAYER FOR HUMILITY

From William Law—The Spirit of Prayer, Pt. 2. p. 124.

I will here give you an infallible touchstone, that will try all to the truth. It is this: retire from the world and all conversation, only for one month; neither write, nor read, nor debate anything with yourself; stop all the former workings of your heart and mind: and, with all the strength of your heart, stand all this month, as continually as you can, in the following form of prayer to God. Offer it frequently on your knees; but whether sitting, walking, or standing, be always inwardly longing, and earnestly praying this one prayer to God: 'That of His great goodness He would make known to you, and take from your heart, every kind and form and degree of Pride, whether it be from evil spirits, or your own corrupt nature; and that He would awaken in you the deepest depth and truth of that Humility, which can make you capable of His light and Holy Spirit.' Reject every thought, but that of waiting and praying in this matter from the bottom of your heart, with such truth and earnestness, as people in torment wish to pray and be delivered from it. ...If you can and will give yourself up in truth and sincerity to this spirit of prayer, I will venture to affirm that, if you had twice as many evil spirits in you as Mary Magdalene had, they will all be cast out of you, and you will be forced with her to weep tears of love at the feet of the holy Jesus.

www.ingramcontent.com/pod-product-compliance
Lightning Source LLC
Chambersburg PA
CBHW030332080526
44584CB00012B/833